D0772604

MYTHOLOGY and
LEGENDS around
the WORLD

McKenzie Co. Public Library
112 2nd Ave. NE
Watford City, ND 58854
701-444-3785
librarian@co.mckenzie.nd.us

# Early American Legends and Folktales

Edited by Joanne Randolph

Cavendish
Square

New York

Published in 2018 by Cavendish Square Publishing, LLC
243 5th Avenue, Suite 136, New York, NY 10016

Copyright © 2018 by Cavendish Square Publishing, LLC

First Edition

No part of this publication may be reproduced, stored in a retrieval system, or transmitted in any form or by any means—electronic, mechanical, photocopying, recording, or otherwise—without the prior permission of the copyright owner. Request for permission should be addressed to Permissions, Cavendish Square Publishing, 243 5th Avenue, Suite 136, New York, NY 10016. Tel (877) 980-4450; fax (877) 980-4454.

Website: cavendishsq.com

This publication represents the opinions and views of the author based on his or her personal experience, knowledge, and research. The information in this book serves as a general guide only. The author and publisher have used their best efforts in preparing this book and disclaim liability rising directly or indirectly from the use and application of this book.

All websites were available and accurate when this book was sent to press.

Cataloging-in-Publication Data

Names: Randolph, Joanne, editor.
Title: Early American legends and folktales / edited by Joanne Randolph.
Description: New York : Cavendish Square Publishing, 2018. | Series: Mythology and legends around the world | Includes bibliographical references and index.
Identifiers: ISBN 9781502632838 (library bound) | ISBN 9781502634504 (pbk.) | ISBN 9781502633118 (ebook)
Subjects: LCSH: Tales--United States--Juvenile literature. | Legends--United States--Juvenile literature. | United States--Folklore--Juvenile literature.
Classification: LCC GR105.R36 2018 | DDC 398.20973--dc23

Editorial Director: David McNamara
Editor: Caitlyn Miller
Copy Editor: Rebecca Rohan
Associate Art Director: Amy Greenan
Designer: Megan Mette
Production Coordinator: Karol Szymczuk
Photo Research: J8 Media

"Tales and Lore" by Kimberly N. Ruffin from *Footsteps* Magazine (May 2006)
"Ghost Ships" by Charlene Brusso from *Appleseeds* Magazine (October 2011)
"The Legend of Black Sam and the Good Ship Whydah" by Kenneth J. Kinkor from *Cobblestone* Magazine (June 1993)
"Did He or Didn't He?" by Leslie Anderson Morales from *Appleseeds* Magazine (February 2004)
"The Myth of Paul Revere's Ride" by Eric Arnesen from *Calliope* Magazine (June 2011)
"The Stranger at the Dance" retold by Robert D. San Souci from *Appleseeds* Magazine (March 2008)
"Watch Out for The Boogeyman!" by Kerry Manzo from *Appleseeds* Magazine (October 2011)
"John Henry: Man vs. Machine" retold by Robert San Souci from *Faces* Magazine (March 2011)
"The Legend of the Line" by Eileen Wellnicki from *Cobblestone* Magazine (March 1982)
"The Phantom Scout: A western legend retold" by Richard J. Silberg from *Cobblestone* Magazine (October 1981)

All articles © by Carus Publishing Company. Reproduced with permission.

All Cricket Media material is copyrighted by Carus Publishing Company, d/b/a Cricket Media, and/or various authors and illustrators. Any commercial use or distribution of material without permission is strictly prohibited. Please visit http://www.cricketmedia.com/info/licensing2 for licensing and http://www.cricketmedia.com for subscriptions.

The photographs in this book are used by permission and through the courtesy of: Cover Ivy Close Images/Alamy Stock Photo; p. 4 Pinkcandy/Shutterstock.com; p. 7 Werner Forman/UIG/Getty Images; p. 8 Look and Learn/Bridgeman Images; p. 11 Hulton Archive/Getty Images; p. 12, 15 Portland Press Herald/Getty Images; p. 16, 50-51 Everett Historical/Shutterstock.com; p. 19 Archive Photos/Getty Images; p. 20 Nathaniel Currier/Wikimedia Commons/File:Boston Tea Party Currier colored.jpg/Public Domain; p. 23 Hulton Archive/Getty Images; p. 24-25 Ed Vebell/Archive Photos/Getty Images; p. 26-27 Bettmann/Getty Images; p. 28 Everett Collection/Alamy Stock Photo; p. 32 Photomara/Shutterstock.com; p. 35 Samuel Putnam Avery Collection/NYPL; p. 36 Zuma/Alamy Stock Photo; p. 38 Detroit Publishing Company/Wikimedia Commons/The Miriam and Ira D. Wallach Division of Art/NYPL/File:The Blue Ridge and C. & O. West from Mason Tunnel, Virginia (NYPL b12647398-74288).tift/Public Domain; p. 40 John Mueller/Wikimedia Commons/File:Big Bend Tunnel John Henry.jpg/CC BY 2.0; p. 42 Detroit Publishing Company/Library of Congress; p. 45 Ken Thomas/Wikimedia Commons/File:John Henry-27527.jpg/Public Domain; p. 46 Dean Fikar/Shutterstock.com; p. 49 MPI/Archive Photos/Getty Images; p. 50 Everett Historical/Shutterstock.com; p. 54 Oomka/Shutterstock.com; p. 57 Mark Skalny/Shutterstock.com; p. 58 GraphicaArtis/Archive Photos/Getty Images.

Printed in the United States of America

# Contents

# Early American Tales and Lore

**B**efore the days of television, DVDs, computers, and smartphones, people used a broad range of creative tools to teach and to entertain. These methods included **folklore**, which means the teachings ("lore") of a group of people ("folk"). For folklore to survive, it must be told and retold in ways that not only capture the attention of those who listen but also inspires them to spread the tales.

Peoples throughout the world have their own folklore, with stories about everything from animals and historical and mythical people to imaginary figures. Riddles, proverbs, **myths**, stories, **legends**, and jokes all contribute to a culture's folklore. Because folklore is older than writing itself, it is considered oral **tradition**; that is, customs that are shared out loud. Through oral traditions, which

*Opposite*: The story of Paul Bunyan, an enormous lumberjack with a giant blue ox for a pet, is one of America's most memorable folktales.

continue even today, people reflect on the world and learn about community values, hopes, and history. Oral traditions from many different geographic and cultural areas came into contact with each other in early America: people of African, European, and Native American backgrounds heard stories that were new to them.

Native Americans told creation stories that often linked humans with animals such as the coyote and the eagle. European tales made connections between humans and a hidden world of imaginary beings such as leprechauns and fairies. African folklore shed light on what it means to be human through its animal tales, particularly those involving the leopard and the tortoise. Each group carried with them their own myths, legends, folktales, and stories. As the stories were retold, they sometimes changed and blended, giving a unique picture of life in early America. Let's take a look at some of these fascinating stories.

*Opposite:* This piece of art is called a frontlet and is worn as part of a Kwakiutl chief's headdress. It references the creation myth of the whale and the raven.

# 2 Ghost Ships

Undamaged vessels floating empty in the middle of the ocean ... Cargo ships sunk in storms, only to be spotted years later sailing in the same waters where they went down ... "Bad luck" ships abandoned by their crews ... Sailors have been telling haunted ship tales probably for as long as there have been ships. Here are some of the most famous ones:

◆ The *Flying Dutchman* is a legendary ghost ship cursed to sail on forever. Sailors have been telling this story for more than four hundred years. Seafarers report hearing her crew call out, begging them to carry messages to loved ones back home.

◆ On March 1, 1858, the steamboat *Eliza Battle* caught fire, killing at least twenty-five people. Since then,

*Opposite*: The *Flying Dutchman* is part of several of the *Pirates of the Caribbean* movies. The tale is also the subject of an opera by Richard Wagner.

many people claim to have seen a flaming ship—the ghost of the *Eliza Battle*—on the Tombigbee River, which flows through Mississippi and Alabama.

♦ The *Amazon* seemed cursed from the start. She lost three captains and had one accident after another. Renamed the *Mary Celeste*, she left New York in 1872 bound for Italy. A month later, she was discovered just west of Gibraltar, crewless and silent, still under sail. No survivors were ever found.

♦ In 1931, the *Baychimo* was trapped in ice off Alaska and was abandoned by her crew. For almost forty years, the *Baychimo* was spotted every year or so. Ice or bad weather always prevented anyone from reaching her. Last seen in 1969, this "Ghost Ship of the Arctic" may still be out there, drifting silently in the cold.

♦ The most famous ghost ship of the Great Lakes is the *Edmund Fitzgerald*. This ore freighter disappeared on Lake Superior during a sudden snow **squall** on November 10, 1975. Though never recovered, she has been sighted many times since.

Many stories set on the high seas, like the "Legend of Black Sam," involve pirates' exploits.

## The Legend of Black Sam and the Good Ship *Whydah*

Sam Bellamy was an honest merchant sailor who went to Cape Cod in the spring of 1715 and fell in love with an Eastham girl, Maria Hallet. Sam was strong, bold, and handsome, and Maria loved him dearly. Maria's parents found young Sam likable enough, but they wanted more for their daughter than a penniless sailor could provide, and they forbade the two to wed.

One autumn day, news arrived of the shipwreck of an entire Spanish treasure fleet off the Florida coast. Sam saw his chance to make both a fortune and a marriage. He bid Maria farewell and, together with a few other stouthearted men, set off to **salvage** some of the tons of silver resting on the bottom of the sea.

The cannon from the *Whydah* is now part of an exhibition called "Real Pirates."

But luck was bad, and they found nothing. Sam could not bear the thought of returning empty-handed, so he turned pirate, learning his trade from the aging Benjamin Hornigold. Immediately, he was enormously successful, and he and his crew took more than fifty ships within the year.

## Pirate Dreams

In February 1717, Bellamy spied his dream ship, the *Whydah*, on the horizon. The *Whydah* was fast, and the chase lasted three days. After a token battle, "Black Sam," as he was sometimes called, easily captured the ship. He and his crew transferred their booty and their cannon to their prize, donated their old ship to the defeated captain and crew, and set a course northward.

The romance between Sam and Maria had caused a great **scandal** in Eastham, and Maria had been banished to the cliffs of what is now Wellfleet. There she made a meager living by weaving cloth. She also became a medicine woman, or, as some said, a witch. Yet, the good folk of Eastham who scorned her by day nonetheless crept to her cabin by night to be cured of their ills. It was also by night that Maria walked the cliffs, watching the running lights of passing ships, hoping that one might be carrying Sam back home to her.

The big ship had come from the south with a fleet of lesser pirate vessels trailing in its wake. It was laden with plunder: gold dust and ivory from Guinea; sugar and indigo from Jamaica; expensive goods hijacked from the English; thousands of gold doubloons and silver pieces of eight; and priceless East Indian gems, including a ruby the size of a hen's egg and worth a queen's ransom.

## Tragedy Strikes

As the fleet was cruising northward along the coast of Cape Cod in the late afternoon of April 26, 1717, fog began to roll in. By 10:00 p.m., a storm was on top of the fleet. At about 11:45 p.m., the *Whydah*'s lookout spotted **breakers** ahead and screamed a warning. It was too late. The crew tried to claw its way offshore against the wind, with no luck. Suddenly, the great ship lurched as it ran aground, stern first. Within fifteen minutes, the mainmast had toppled and thirty-foot breakers had pushed the ship off the sandbar and into deeper water, where it quickly **capsized** and broke up.

On that same dark April night, with thundering surf and a howling wind, Maria was walking the cliffs.

Gold recovered from the *Whydah* shipwreck

She heard the dying screams of drowning men (only two would survive) and the last clang of a storm-tossed bell. Then her grief-wracked wails drowned out the wind itself, for she recognized her beloved Sam's voice among the dying. The legend of the *Whydah* brought countless treasure seekers to the coast of Cape Cod over the years, but it wasn't until 1984 that the wreck was finally discovered by Barry Clifford. The items he and his crew have recovered so far are on display in the Whydah Pirate Museum on Cape Cod.

# 3 Did He or Didn't He?

**H**ave you ever heard this story? George Washington's father gave his little boy a hatchet. Eager to try it out, George cut down a cherry tree on the farm. When his father asked George what had happened, the boy answered, "I cannot tell a lie. It was I." His father was so proud of the boy for telling the truth that he did not punish him.

Almost two hundred years ago, Mason Locke Weems wrote that story in a biography for children. He said he heard the story from an old woman who was the Washingtons' neighbor. It was later included in a textbook that schoolchildren read in the 1800s. Years later, people found out that Weems had made up the story.

How about the story that says George Washington threw a silver dollar all the way across the Potomac River? Well, silver dollars didn't exist during George Washington's lifetime. Also, since then, professional

*Opposite*: George Washington was known for his honesty, but it's a myth that he said the words "I cannot tell a lie. It was I."

baseball pitchers have tried to throw small items across the river's narrowest point, and they have not been able to do it.

These two stories are myths. Myths are stories that are often told about heroes and other important people but that don't necessarily tell about something that really happened. Some myths teach values and remind us how to behave properly. Other myths tell about (made-up) adventures. However, myths are usually based on truth, such as the fact that George Washington was known as an honest and strong man.

So why did people make up these two myths about George Washington? Many people believed that George Washington could do things other people could not. He led our nation in its early years of struggle and became our first president. Perhaps Mr. Weems made up the myth about the cherry tree to inspire young people to be honest. What do you think?

# Another Did He or Didn't He: Paul Revere's Ride

By the spring of 1775, the conflict between Great Britain and the citizens of its Massachusetts Bay Colony had

Mason Locke Weems invented the story of George Washington and the cherry tree.

THE DESTRUCTION OF TEA AT BOSTON HARBOR.

The Boston Tea Party was a turning point in colonial history.

grown increasingly tense. Five years earlier, in an effort to punish those resisting their authority, British troops had fired on a crowd in what was called the Boston Massacre. Then, in 1773, colonists had protested the Tea Act with the so-called Boston Tea Party, a dumping of tea in Boston's harbor. The British responded by closing the port.

Matters came to a head in 1775 as the British prepared to attack armed colonists. The situation worsened in April of that year. That's when General Thomas Gage, the soldier who commanded the British garrison in Boston, dispatched 1,000 troops to Concord, Massachusetts, to seize the colonists' weapons.

## A Tale Begins

One version of what happened that day in April was made famous seventy-five years later, in 1861, when Henry Wadsworth Longfellow published "Paul Revere's Ride" in the *Atlantic Monthly* magazine. The poem immortalized the feats of one particular Bostonian on the eve of the American Revolution: "Listen my children and you shall hear / Of the midnight ride of Paul Revere," wrote Longfellow. According to the poem, in April 1775, Revere said to a friend, "If the British march / By land or sea from the town to-night, / Hang a lantern aloft in the belfry arch / Of the North Church tower as a signal light,—One if by land, and two if by sea."

In Longfellow's telling, Revere waited on the opposite shore, "Ready to ride and spread the alarm / Through every Middlesex village and farm / For the country folk to be up and to arm." The signal came—two lights. Revere sprang into action on his horse, "fearless and fleet. The fate of a nation was riding that night; / And the spark struck out by that steed, in his flight, / Kindled the land into flame with its heat."

The Paul Revere of Longfellow's poem spread the word to the communities outside of Boston. "And so through the night went his cry of alarm / To every Middlesex village and far … / A Cry of defiance, and not of fear."

Revere reached the towns of Lexington and Concord after midnight. "Through all our history, to the last," wrote Longfellow, "In the hour of darkness and peril and need, / The people will waken and listen to hear … the midnight message of Paul Revere."

## The Truth Comes Out

As it turns out, Longfellow's poem contained a good deal of fiction. Paul Revere, the son of a French immigrant and a prominent Boston silversmith, was not the single hero of Longfellow's imagination. Paul Revere's ride "was truly a collective effort," Revere's recent biographer, David Hackett Fischer, tells us. Revere "would be very much surprised by his modern image as the lone rider of the Revolution." Not only did many other messengers travel by horse to warn neighboring towns, Revere's actual assignment had been to warn two prominent

Paul Revere lived from 1735 to 1818. He did warn colonists that the British were coming, but he was not the only person to do so.

Paul Revere rode through
Massachusetts on April 18, 1775.

colonists—Samuel Adams
and John Hancock—that
the British military was
on its way. Further, after
successfully warning Adams
and Hancock, Revere
was temporarily taken
prisoner by the British.
(He then escaped.)

The Battles of Lexington
and Concord that followed
the ride of the many
messengers was the
beginning of the American
War for Independence.
Longfellow may have created
the legend of Paul Revere,
but the credit for alerting the
colonists to the coming of
British troops deserves to be
shared by the many colonists
who risked their lives on that
night—and on many that followed.

The Battles of Lexington and Concord were the official start of the American Revolution. They took place the day after Paul Revere's ride.

# 4 Scary Legends

The following is a folktale from the Southwest about a charming and mysterious stranger who attends a dance and turns out to be not at all what he seems. However, this same story is told in many different places. As with so many folktales, it contains a lesson. "The Stranger at the Dance" cautions children to obey their parents and to stay away from places that might be dangerous.

## The Stranger at the Dance

Cecilia was a very smart girl, but she was careless and stubborn. She did what she wanted, no matter what her parents said.

One day, her mother said, "Cecilia, I must be away tonight. So you must look after your little brother, Julio."

*Opposite*: Couples dance in Brownsville, Texas, in 1942.

"But my friends have asked me to go with them to the dance hall tonight," the girl protested.

Her mother warned her, "I forbid you to go. You must tend your little brother. Besides, the dance hall is no place for a young woman. El Diablo, the devil, waits for the innocent in such places."

But Cecilia paid no attention. When her mother left, Cecilia, in her fanciest dress, slipped away to the dance hall. She carried her drowsy little brother with her.

When she reached the place, she found it filled with lanterns and streamers, and crowded with young people from miles around. Quickly, she placed sleeping Julio under a small table in a corner of the room. The band began to play, and she hurried to join her friends.

Cecilia was talking and laughing with her friends about the foolishness of their parents. Suddenly, the other young women fell silent as a stranger approached. Turning, Cecilia saw the most handsome man she had ever seen. He wore an elegant outfit of black, heavily embroidered with fanciful designs. His pants were tucked into polished boots inlaid with mother-of-pearl.

He bowed low and smiled, showing perfect teeth.

All the girls began to giggle and flutter their handkerchiefs and lashes. But the stranger's eyes swept past the others and came to rest on Cecilia's lovely face. To her annoyance, she realized her face was burning. But the man's smile only grew wider. He took Cecilia's hand in his own. The stranger asked politely, "Señorita, will you dance with me?"

Delighting in the jealous looks from her friends, Cecilia followed the handsome fellow onto the dance floor. Dazzled by his winning smile and the sweet words he whispered into her ear, the girl began to dream that she would soon be dancing at her own wedding. Oh! How she would tease her mother, whose silly warnings would have kept her from the dance hall and her chance at true happiness.

Just before midnight, the stranger excused himself and retreated to a corner of the room. He bent down to tuck in one pant cuff that had come free. With his back to the room, he quickly removed his boot. At that moment, Julio, who had awakened and was watching from beneath the table, cried out, "¡Mira—pata de gallo! Look—a rooster foot!"

Bellowing, the stranger whirled around, looking angrily for the one who had betrayed him. Now everyone could see that, indeed, his foot was scaly and clawed— just like a rooster's. Cecilia gave a shriek. The lights went out. As people shouted and jostled each other in the dark, Cecilia screamed a second time, and then a third.

When the lanterns flared into light again, Julio knelt beside his sister. She lay face down on the floor, moaning. People rushed to her aid and turned her over. Cecilia kept her hands pressed to her face, sobbing. At last, one of the older women pulled Cecilia's fingers free of her face. Then she gasped, as did everyone else in the room: Cecilia's beautiful face had been clawed almost to ribbons.

A search was made for the stranger, but there was no trace of him to be found. The bit of wooden floor where he had last been standing was burned black, and there was a stink of sulfur in the air. The frightened partygoers had no doubt about his identity. "El Diablo," they whispered to each other in shocked voices, "the devil."

Cecilia's dance partner scorched the floor, then disappeared.

# Watch Out for the Boogeyman!

"Sleep my baby,
Sleep, baby, do!
The boogeyman's coming
And he will take you.
Sleep my baby,
Sleep, baby, do!
The boogeyman's coming
And he will eat you!"

—*A traditional Mexican American lullaby*

Young people all around the world are sometimes afraid of monsters in the night. Some have more reasons to be afraid than others. In Mexican American culture, children who misbehave might be told they have some very scary creatures to worry about, as the lullaby above warns.

## El Cucuy

"Behave and go to sleep, or the Cucuy will come and get you," Francisco's mother says with a knowing wink. The boy's eyes grow large, and he wriggles into his bed, pulling the sheets over his eyes. He will sleep, or pretend to sleep, because nothing is more frightening than El Cucuy [el coo-COO-ee].

But who is El Cucuy? As any well-behaved Mexican American kid will tell you, El Cucuy is a small creature with glowing eyes and razor-sharp teeth in a head like a coconut. He hangs from rooftops and lurks under beds, looking for misbehaving children. Francisco may never have seen El Cucuy, but he has heard of the goblin many times before, and he is not eager to feel those razor teeth.

The legend of El Cucuy goes back beyond the Spanish and Portuguese explorers who brought it to the Americas. In parts of the Spanish-speaking world, he is known as El Coco, El Cocu, or El Chamuco. In the southwestern United States, he is always known as El Cucuy, the original boogeyman of Mexican American culture.

## La Llorona

*Oooooooo* … The wind howls outside the window.

"What is that sound, Mama?" Pilar asks.

"That is La Llorona [la yoh-ROH-nah]," her mother says. "She is looking for children to replace the ones she killed."

*Opposite*: A woman and her children come face to face with El Cucuy.

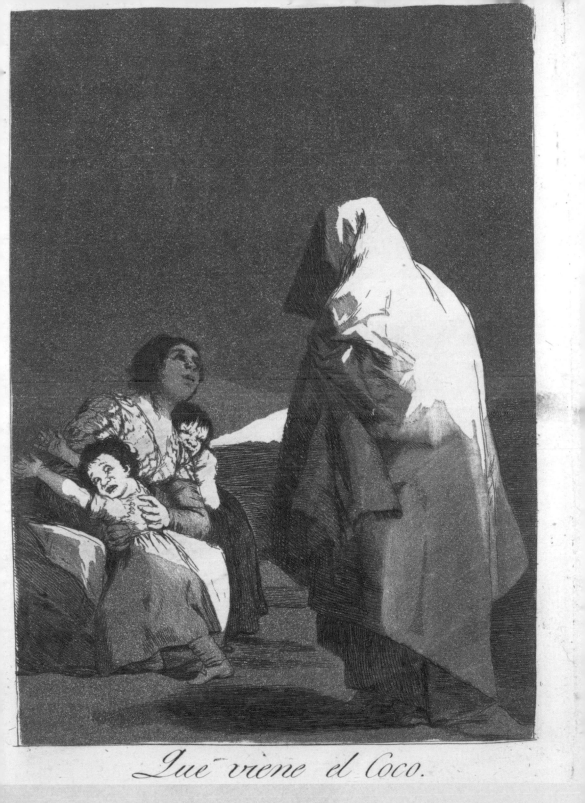

Qué viene el Coco.

It is said that
La Llorona's
grief and regret
killed her.

Pilar doesn't like to go out at night. Even by her mother's side, she clings to the safety of her mother's hand. She knows the tale of La Llorona very well.

La Llorona was once a beautiful woman who married the most handsome man in her village. She was proud of her beauty and thought her husband should be devoted to no one but her. She was jealous of everyone her husband gave attention to. She was even jealous of the attention he gave to his own children!

Soon, La Llorona became convinced that her husband loved her children more than he loved her. In a rage, she led her children to the river and drowned them in its waters. Realizing what she had done, she was so heartbroken that she died instantly of grief.

"To this day," Pilar's mother warns, "La Llorona wanders beside the river after dark, crying for her lost children. If you are out alone after dark, you had better look out, or La Llorona might get you."

71471    THE BLUE RIDGE AND C. & O. WEST FROM MASON TUNNEL, VA.

# John Henry: Man vs. Machine

Folks say lightning flashed and the whole state of Virginia shook the night John Henry was born to Preacher Henry and his wife. The same folks say he weighed forty-four pounds at birth.

Even as a baby, John loved hammering things. By age ten, he could hammer down fence posts like a grown man. At eighteen, he was more than six feet tall, weighed about two hundred pounds, and was strong as a locomotive. When working on the family's small farm, he would hear a distant train whistle and say, "Someday, I'm gonna be a steel driver for the railroad."

## The C&O

John went to West Virginia to realize his dream. He signed on with the Chesapeake & Ohio—called the C&O—railroad crew, working on the Big Bend Tunnel. One and a

*Opposite:* John Henry worked on the C&O railroad crew.

The historical marker for the Big Bend Tunnel commemorates John Henry.

quarter miles long, it would cut through a mountain and become the longest railroad tunnel in America.

John Henry was hired as a driver—someone who hammered a steel drill into the rock to make an opening for blasting powder. His every blow drove the drill an inch deeper into solid rock. The work was hard, and the days were hot, but John loved the idea that his hammering was helping make a tunnel through which trains would soon roar. His boss boasted, "He's my finest driver. I'd match him against any man."

Though tough, John had a tender heart and fell in love with Lucy, who worked as a maid. She was short to his tall, coffee and cream to his ebony—but while she seemed soft, she was a steel-driving woman from a family of railroad workers. She could lay down rails second only to John Henry, if she had a mind to.

They were soon married and lived in one of the little wooden shanties that housed the railroad workers. The whole crew turned out for the wedding. They bought John a new twenty-pound hammer and gave Lucy a flapjack turner big enough to flip hotcakes the size of wagon wheels.

# The Iron Monster

Word reached the tunneling crew that the owners of the C&O railroad were thinking of buying a newly invented steam drill to replace many workers. John Henry and the other men laughed and called it "the iron monster." But the drill's inventor insisted, "My machine will drill a hole faster than any ten men!" Then John began to worry that he might lose his job and his and Lucy's dream of buying a farm. And it bothered him to think that folks would say the tunnel was dug by a machine, not a good, honest man's work.

Railroad workers use steam drills in the early 1900s.

So John went to his boss and said, "You tell everyone, 'I've got a man who can swing two twenty-pound hammers. He'll beat that steam drill down and prove that a man is better than any iron monster.' But you gotta promise, if I win, you'll keep all the men working until the Big Bend Tunnel is finished."

The boss agreed to a thirty-minute contest. If the machine outdrilled John Henry, the C&O would buy it and fire the workers. But if John Henry won, they would pay him $100, and he and the other men could keep their jobs.

Lucy was worried, and she tried to get him to give up his plan. But John kissed her and said, "The men are countin' on me. And with that money, we can buy our farm. Besides, a man ain't nothin' but a man. I gotta prove that no machine can drill better than a sledgehammer and steel in an honest man's hand."

# The Contest

The next day, the man-giant and the steam drill lined up side by side, near the end of the tunnel, while a big crowd gathered inside. The boss dropped his flag and the contest began.

At first the steam-powered drill pulled ahead.

But this only made John Henry slam his hammer down faster. By the time the contest was halfway over, John Henry's spikes were biting just as deep as the machine's, while the men cheered.

Soon John's twenty-pounders rose and fell so fast they were almost invisible. The sweat poured down his face, and he grunted as he strained to lift his hammers. Still John slammed away. And he smiled when he saw the steam drill begin to overheat and shake.

John pulled farther ahead. His muscles were aching, and the rock seemed to grow harder, but this only made him pound more forcefully. Just before the boss yelled, "Time!," the mechanical spike driver shook and wheezed and ground to a halt.

But John Henry could not slow down at first. He drove his spike several inches deeper, then suddenly fell to the ground. The men carried him out of the tunnel and laid him with his head in Lucy's lap.

This statue of John Henry is in Summers County, West Virginia.

"Lucy," he gasped. "Did I beat that steam drill?"

"You did," she said, her tears falling like cool rain on his burning face.

"Oh, Lucy, I hear a roarin' in my head, like a locomotive rushin' down the tracks," John said. Then his soul boarded the train that only he could see. While John Henry died that hot July day, his story became a part of railroad legend. Wherever a train speeds over the tracks, some part of John Henry rides the rails with it.

# 6 The Legend of the Line

I t was in the evening of the second day of March in 1836 that a band of thirty-two men from the town of Gonzales, Texas, rode into the Alamo. The men had ridden nearly seventy miles, led by Captain John W. Smith and Captain Albert Martin. Both men had left the Alamo earlier carrying the news that the fort was under **siege**. The captains had managed to guide the Gonzales volunteers past the 1,800 Mexican soldiers of General Santa Anna that surrounded the fort. The arrival of the thirty-two men lifted the spirits of everyone in the Alamo except Colonel William B. Travis, the commanding officer.

## Stacked Odds

Colonel Travis had sent out an impassioned plea for reinforcements. His letter had been addressed "To the

*Opposite*: Today, the Alamo gets more than two million visitors a year.

People of Texas and All Americans in the World." The response was thirty-two volunteers. Thirty-two when he expected a hundred farmers, when he needed soldiers. Travis knew that a few more men were better than none. But still he wished for the forces of Colonel Fannin, commander of the town of Goliad.

Travis decided the time had come to be honest with his men about their situation. The evening after the volunteers arrived, he called a meeting in the Alamo courtyard. The fort's 183 defenders were an unusual group. Some were farmers, dressed in simple homespun clothes. Others, like Davy Crockett, were men of the backwoods who dressed in buckskin. The youngest was a fifteen-year-old youth from Gonzales; the oldest, a fifty-five-year-old Virginian. Travis looked over the group, then he began to speak.

"Men, there comes a time when all must stand against tyranny. Yesterday we received a band of valiant men from Gonzales. I had hoped that by now Colonel Fannin's forces from Goliad would arrive. I know now that they will not. It is our small band against Santa Anna's army. I cannot demand that you stay to fight—to die."

*Opposite:* The odds were stacked against Colonel Travis's men, but they fought bravely.

Legend has it that Colonel Travis drew a line on the ground. Those willing to fight crossed that line.

Travis paused and drew his sword. With it, he drew a line in the dirt in front of him. Then he continued: "I draw this line to give you a choice. If you will stay and help defend this fort to the death, then cross this line and show your support. I will not ask you to stay if you believe you cannot. If you wish to surrender or to try to escape, I would suggest that you do it now, for time grows short. I believe the assault will come soon."

There was a moment of silence. Then a young man crossed the line. He was Tapley Holland, twenty-four years old, born in Ohio, and a resident of Grimes County, Texas. He was followed quickly by others who were willing to give their lives for what they believed in. In a moment, the line had started to fade under the boots of the men crossing it.

James Bowie, the original commander of the Alamo, was too ill to walk across the line. He asked that his cot be carried across. The line Travis drew was crossed by every man in the Alamo—except one.

All eyes turned to the lone man by the campfire. He was Louis Moses Rose, a Frenchman. Rose looked at his old friend, James Bowie, who gave a slight nod to show that he understood. Rose stood and moved quickly into the shadows. He vaulted to the top of the wall, glanced back at the others, then jumped to the outside of the fort, landing in a patch of cactus.

Picking himself up, Rose began creeping in the direction of the river. Limping slightly, he followed it downstream, slipping quietly between the soldiers at the villages of La Villita and Bejar. Shivering a bit, the small Frenchman continued to follow the path of the San Antonio River downstream until, finally, he reached the safety of the open country.

During the next several days, Rose managed to elude General Santa Anna's army and the Comanche and Apache Indians. He was also able to cross the open **prairie** on foot with few provisions. He eventually found his way to the home of a family named Zuber. Rose told the tale of his escape to the family. Their young son, William Zuber, remembered the story all his life, and it is mostly from him that we have the accounts of the legend of the line. It may be that Colonel William Barrett Travis never drew that famous line, but the story became a part of Alamo history just the same.

# 7 The Phantom Scout

L egends of hard-riding, faithful messengers, killed while on an important mission, are still to be heard in the West. In Wyoming, a high and windswept land, such stories find an especially appropriate setting.

## A Ride to Remember

Charles was a young man who lived with his parents in their country home, located several miles from the limits of Cheyenne. Every day he would go to work in Cheyenne aboard a fine saddle horse. Usually he would return home in time for dinner, but one night, he decided to take in some entertainment in town.

He went to a show that ended late, so it was near midnight when Charles finally began his ride home. The moon was full and its chalk-white light illuminated

*Opposite*: Wyoming is the setting for many exciting legends and folktales about the West.

the road and the surrounding prairie. Clouds would occasionally obscure the moon's light, casting eerie shadows across the landscape. This made Charles a bit nervous. He rode as quickly as his horse would take him over the road. Suddenly, Charles discovered that he was not the only one riding at this hour. He could see clearly another horseman riding like mad across the nearby plain. The rider was bent low over his mount, urging the horse to ride as swiftly as possible.

Charles thought that the person on the horse was in trouble. He decided to see if there was any way that he could help the man. Charles noted that the angle at which the other rider was approaching would bring the two men together at some point down the road, if he rode as swiftly as possible. Charles dug his spurs into his horse, urging him on to meet the troubled rider.

## A Chilling Mystery

When Charles got to the spot, he reared his horse around and prepared to offer his aid. To his surprise the rider did not slacken his speed at all when he approached Charles and his horse. Instead, he sped by in a rush of icy wind that caused Charles's horse to rear up and snort wildly. The next thing Charles knew, both he and his horse stood

Charles used his spurs to encourage his horse to go faster. Yet he still couldn't catch the other horseman.

in a ditch by the roadside, his horse trembling in fear.

It took some time before Charles could calm his horse and encourage him to climb out of the ditch and chase the other horseman. When he finally did, it was too late. The other rider was nowhere in sight, despite the fact that it was a clear night and the prairie stretched out for miles in all directions. Surely no horse, no matter how swift he was, could have covered that ground in such a short period of time, Charles thought.

It was then that fear hit Charles. He realized that he had never heard any sound from the other rider. No hoof beats, no hard breathing. And his own horse was

badly frightened. Charles had heard that animals were particularly sensitive to the presence of (and at this thought, Charles hesitated) ... ghosts.

Charles was too embarrassed to say anything about this episode to his own friends, but he did mention the incident to some of his father's friends, some of whom were original settlers in those parts. They told him similar stories. They said the apparition was the ghost of an old Pony Express rider, killed by Indians while he was carrying a note warning settlers about an uprising. Unable to rest with his mission unfulfilled, he continued to ride night after night, trying to deliver the message to a group of **phantom** villagers who waited in vain to receive it.

*Opposite*: A Pony Express rider in the 1860s

# Glossary

**breakers**  Heavy ocean waves that break on the shore or shoals, also called whitecaps.

**capsized**  Tipped over in the water.

**folklore**  The traditional beliefs, customs, and stories of a community, passed through the generations by word of mouth.

**legends**  Traditional stories that may be thought of as historical or factual but that cannot be proven.

**myths**  Legends or stories that typically concern the origins of a people or explain natural or societal phenomena and will often include gods or supernatural beings.

**phantom**  A ghost.

**prairie**  A large, open area with grass.

**salvage**  The rescue of a ship or its cargo that has been lost at sea.

**scandal** An action or event regarded as morally or legally wrong, which causes people to become upset.

**siege** A military operation where forces surround a building or town, cutting off access to vital supplies and resources, in hopes of forcing the people inside to surrender.

**squall** A sudden, violent storm or gust of wind.

**tradition** A passing of customs or ways of doing things from generation to generation.

# Further Information

## Books

Hamilton, Virginia. *The People Could Fly: American Black Folktales*. New York: Knopf Books for Young Readers, 1993.

Osborne, Mary Pope. *American Tall Tales*. New York: Knopf Books for Young Readers, 1991.

Yolen, Jane, and Heidi E. Y. Stemple. *The Mary Celeste: An Unsolved Mystery from History*. New York: Simon & Schuster Books for Young Readers, 2002.

## Websites

**American Folklore**

http://americanfolklore.net/folklore/myths-legends/

Read hundreds of American folktales, myths, and legends on this website created by author S. E. Schlosser.